MARGATE CITY PUBLIC LIBRARY

8100 ATLANTIC AVENUE

MARGATE CITY, NJ 08402

(609) 822-4700

www.margatelibrary.org

1. Most items may be checked out for two weeks and renewed for the same period. Additional restrictions may apply to high-demand items.

2. A fine is charged for each day material is not returned according to the above rule. No material will be issued to any person incurring such a fine until it has been paid.

3. All damage to material beyond reasonable wear and all losses shall be paid for.

4. Each borrower is responsible for all items checked out on his/her library card and for all fines accruing on the same.

JAN   2017

Creepy Creatures

WITCHES

Big Buddy Books
An Imprint of Abdo Publishing
abdopublishing.com

Sarah Tieck

abdopublishing.com

Published by Abdo Publishing, a division of ABDO, PO Box 398166, Minneapolis, Minnesota 55439.
Copyright © 2016 by Abdo Consulting Group, Inc. International copyrights reserved in all countries. No part
of this book may be reproduced in any form without written permission from the publisher. Big Buddy Books™
is a trademark and logo of Abdo Publishing.

Printed in the United States of America, North Mankato, Minnesota.
042015
092015

THIS BOOK CONTAINS
RECYCLED MATERIALS

Cover Photo: Virgil Apger/Getty Images.
Interior Photos: © AF archive/Alamy (p. 19); ASSOCIATED PRESS (pp. 17, 21, 23, 27, 29); © Nancy Carter/North Wind
    Picture Archives (p. 11); Gamma-Rapho via Getty Images (pp. 20, 25); ©iStockphoto.com (pp. 5, 7, 13, 17, 30);
    © North Wind Picture Archives (p. 20); © Photos 12/Alamy (p. 22); Shutterstock.com (pp. 9, 25); Universal
    History Archive/Getty Images (p. 15).

Coordinating Series Editor: Rochelle Baltzer
Contributing Editors: Megan M. Gunderson, Bridget O'Brien, Marcia Zappa
Graphic Design: Jenny Christensen

Library of Congress Cataloging-in-Publication Data

Tieck, Sarah, 1976- author.
  Witches / Sarah Tieck.
      pages cm. -- (Creepy creatures)
  ISBN 978-1-62403-769-6
  1. Witches--Juvenile literature. I. Title.
  BF1566.T48 2016
  133.4'3--dc23
                              2015004212

Contents

Creepy Witches

People love to tell spooky stories, especially about creepy creatures such as witches. They describe their cackling laughs. They guess what horrid **potions** are in their **cauldrons**. And, they report seeing them flying on broomsticks during a full moon.

Witches have appeared in books, stories, plays, television shows, and movies. But are they real, or the stuff of **legend**? Let's find out more about witches, and you can decide for yourself!

Did you know?

People imagine witches meeting in spooky places, such as in a graveyard or around a fire.

Legendary witches are often scary, ugly, and evil!

Scary Stories

People usually think of witches as old women with wrinkles and long, messy hair. They have long noses with warts. They wear black clothes and pointy black hats. Other times, witches are young and beautiful.

Stories describe witches as living alone. Witches brew **potions** in black **cauldrons**. They use plants and even animals, such as frogs. Some simply say special words or point their fingers to cast **spells**.

Did you know?

Witches often have large, old books with instructions for potions and spells.

A witch's house in a story or movie often has dried plants and other unusual objects used to make potions.

Witches don't just use magic to fly on brooms. Some use it to change shape! Black cats are believed to be a witch's spirit in animal form. So, a black cat crossing your path is thought to bring bad luck.

In many stories, witches use magic to make bad things happen. They cause storms, accidents, and diseases.

Legends tell of witches changing into animal forms including cats, dogs, snakes, and owls.

9

Around the World

For centuries, people from many **cultures** have told stories of witches, magic, and sorcery. Most describe witches as having **supernatural** powers.

In Native American **legends**, witches change shape and are active at night. For example, Navajo skinwalkers met after dark wearing the skins of dead animals. They performed evil **spells**.

The Navajo protected themselves against witches using sand paintings.

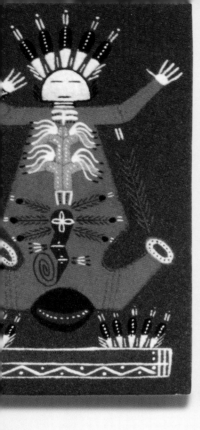
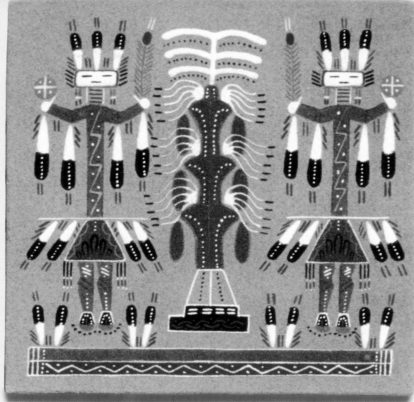
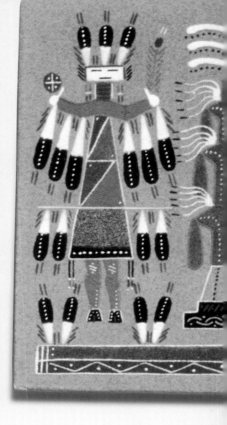

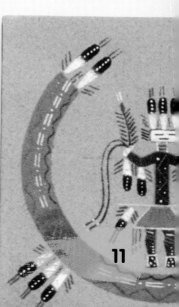

11

In some parts of the world, the belief in witches and witchcraft is still strong. Just like in stories, people believe bad things are caused by witches. People may even harm those they fear to be witches.

Did you know?

People believe some wit are unaware of their po the problems they cause

In Africa and Asia, some natural disasters, such as floods, storms, or wildfires, are thought to be the result of witchcraft.

Witch Hunts

Around the AD 1000s, Europeans began to fear witches. Stories spread that witches had evil powers. Witches were said to change shapes, meet secretly at night, and kill people. People feared that witches would hurt them or use them in **potions**!

By the 1700s, more than 100,000 people had been put in jail for being witches. Many were punished for crimes they did not do. Some historians believe up to half were put to death.

People were very afraid of witches and what they might do. So, those accused of being witches were put on trial and spent time in jail.

Witch hunts also happened in the United States. The Salem witch trials took place in 1692 near Boston, Massachusetts. They began when a group of young girls said three women were witches and were doing evil things.

Soon, more people were accused. In all, 20 people were put to death as witches. Today, people believe they were not guilty. The people of Salem likely acted in this way because they were so afraid of evil.

There is a special memorial in Salem, Massachusetts, that honors the victims of the Salem witch trials.

Many old buildings can be seen today in Salem. One is Judge Jonathan Corwin's house, known as the Witch House. He was one of the town leaders during the trials.

Witch House

Good or Evil?

In many stories, witches are evil. They trick and trap people. They even kidnap children. Good often fights evil in these stories. People have to find ways to break a witch's harmful **spell**.

Yet in other stories, witches are good. They help crops grow, heal sickness, or see into the future. Sometimes they use their spells to grant wishes.

Did you know?

In some stories, witches are much older than they may appear. They use spells to look younger.

In 1939, Billie Burke (*left*) played Glinda the Good Witch of the North in *The Wizard of Oz*. Judy Garland (*right*) played Dorothy.

Grimm's Fairy Tales

Witches are part of many Grimm Brothers fairy tales, such as "Hansel and Gretel."

Hermione Granger

In the Harry Potter books and movies, Hermione Granger is a witch. Her parents are muggles, or non-magic humans. She is known for being skilled and smart.

Witches in Pop Culture

The Wicked Witch of the West

In 1900, L. Frank Baum's book *The Wonderful Wizard of Oz* came out. After the 1939 movie, the story's Wicked Witch became famous for her green skin and her power over flying monkeys.

Did you know?

In Roald Dahl's book *The Witches*, a witch turns the main character into a mouse!

Angelina Jolie played Maleficent in the 2014 movie. Some of the child actors were afraid of the scary makeup she wore!

Maleficent

The 2014 movie *Maleficent* retells the famous story of *Sleeping Beauty*. In it, Maleficent is a fairy that flies, has powers, and casts **spells** like a witch.

Ursula

The sea witch in *The Little Mermaid* uses magic to steal Ariel's voice. She also changes shape and size.

The Evil Queen

In *Snow White*, this witch changes her appearance and uses a magic mirror.

23

Wizards

Wizards are males who have magical powers. Like witches, they use **potions** and **spells**. J.K. Rowling's Harry Potter books are about a boy who discovers he is a wizard. Harry Potter attends a special school to learn to use his magical powers.

J.R.R. Tolkien's Lord of the Rings books include a powerful wizard named Gandalf. He uses his magical staff to light dark passages and fight enemies. Saruman is also a powerful wizard. But, he helps the dark forces because he wants even more power.

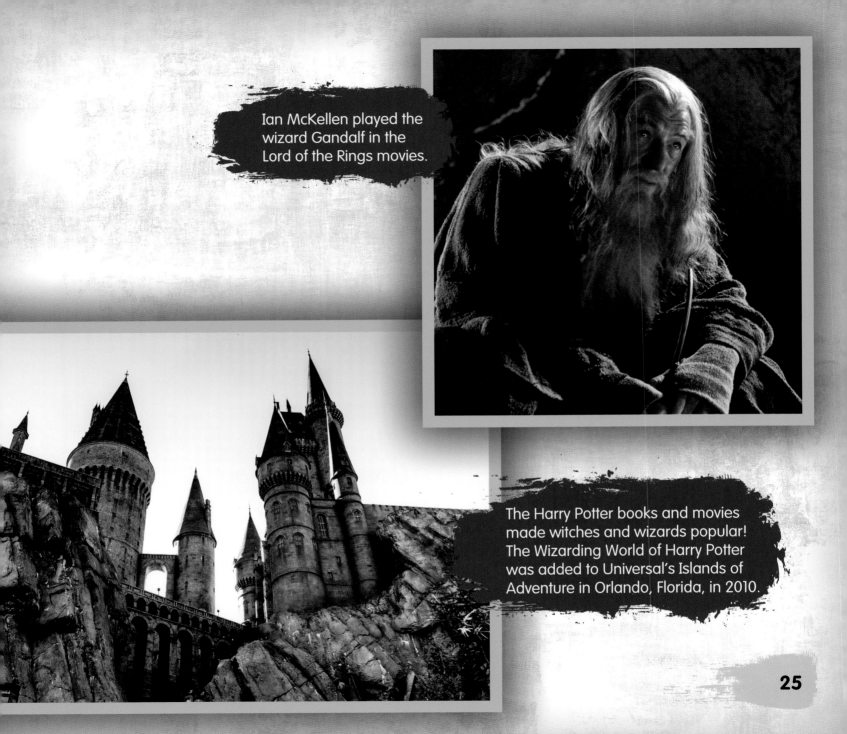

Ian McKellen played the wizard Gandalf in the Lord of the Rings movies.

The Harry Potter books and movies made witches and wizards popular! The Wizarding World of Harry Potter was added to Universal's Islands of Adventure in Orlando, Florida, in 2010.

Fact or Fiction?

Belief in witches is still part of some **cultures**. And, people who practice the Wicca religion are known as witches. They focus on nature and seasons. They use plants and herbs to make healing **potions**.

People once thought the powers of potions were magic. This scared them, because they worried the potions might be harmful. Today, people know the healing powers come from the **chemicals** in plants and herbs.

Did you know?

People may drink or eat a potion. Or, they may breathe in its smoke.

Some potions involve paper, fire, and spices.

What Do You Think?

So, what do you think about witches? Do they still send a chill up your spine? It can be fun to tell spooky stories of witches or to dress as witches on Halloween.

It is also interesting to learn about witches, past and present. Knowing what is true and what is made up is powerful. Whether you read **fiction** about witches or discover their real-life history, you are in for an interesting journey.

People dress up as witches for fun at Halloween. They wear makeup, wigs, and special clothes.

29

Let's Talk

What examples of witches and wizards can you think of?

If you were a witch or wizard, what powers would you like to have?

Would you cast **spells**? Would you be a good witch or a creepy witch?

How do you think it would feel to be part of a witch hunt?

If you were to write a story about a witch, what would your witch look like?

Can you think of any other people, places, or things that are different in stories than they are in real life?

Glossary

cauldron a large pot.

chemical (KEH-mih-kuhl) a substance that can cause reactions and changes.

culture (KUHL-chuhr) the arts, beliefs, and ways of life of a group of people.

fiction stories that are not real.

legend an old story that many believe, but cannot be proven true.

potion (POH-shuhn) a mixture of liquids.

spell words with magic powers.

supernatural unable to be explained by science or nature.

Websites

To learn more about Creepy Creatures, visit **booklinks.abdopublishing.com**. These links are routinely monitored and updated to provide the most current information available.

Index